Songs of Sigma Alpha Epsilon

Editor

William C. Levere

Alpha Editions

This edition published in 2020

ISBN : 9789354044083

Design and Setting By
Alpha Editions
www.alphaedis.com
email - alphaedis@gmail.com

As per information held with us this book is in Public Domain. This book is a reproduction of an important historical work. Alpha Editions uses the best technology to reproduce historical work in the same manner it was first published to preserve its original nature. Any marks or number seen are left intentionally to preserve its true form.

Songs
OF
Sigma Alpha Epsilon

William C. Levere
Editor

Walter Squire
Musical Editor

Published for the Fraternity
1907

Dedication.

This volume is especially dedicated to the three members of the song book committee,

Mr. L. Emerson Warfield, California Alpha

Mr. C. P. Wood, New York Alpha

and more particularly
to the chairman

Mr. Roy H. Monier, Illinois Psi-Omega

FOREWORD.

Twenty years ago members of Sigma Alpha Epsilon were agitating a song book for the fraternity. This agitation has continued ever since. This book is therefore a fulfilment of the various axioms of the strenuous to the effect that continual "knocking" will make a hole in a wall. If on an occasion so happy any attempt were to be made to place the fault for the delay of two decades, the editor would recourse to his previous accusations and pointing to any who have failed to contribute either rhyme or note would Nathan-like exclaim to each "Thou art the man." It is far from his thought though to stir up strife now that the arduous task is done. The very fact that the negligent are not found here is punishment enough for them.

In the work of gathering these songs tributes are due to many from Colorado Chi which did good work along this line many years ago down to the latest song book committee appointed early in 1904, the work of whose chairman, Brother Roy H. Monier, continued until the adoption of the editor's plan by the Supreme Council late in 1905. That plan, now well known to the fraternity, was successful in bringing out a large number of new songs and musical compositions, and made possible the appearance of this volume.

The work of Brother Walter E. Squire as musical editor deserves warmest commendation. For two years he has given much of his time and all of his rare talent to the service of the fraternity. He has brought a musical education of the first order to the work and with his knowledge has united careful and critical judgment. Many similar publications are practically useless, due to the difficulty of the key signatures and accompaniments, but he has avoided this fault by keeping within the more familiar keys and simplifying somewhat the piano parts. Knowing that songs of this character are usually sung in unison, he has placed the melody in the compass common to most male voices, centering between middle 'c' and the octave below. The wise rule of having the melody appear in the first tenor part and to be played by the right hand when piano accompaniments are used, was also adopted. In a few instances where the music is distinctly in quartette style the melody is taken by the baritone.

It is the hope of the editor that much happiness may be brought to Sigma Alpha Epsilon by this book. May every one of our seventy chapters be centers of rousing, joyful song.

With fraternal regards,
WILLIAM C. LEVERE

COPYRIGHT, 1907 BY
WILLIAM C. LEVERE

SING, BROTHERS SING

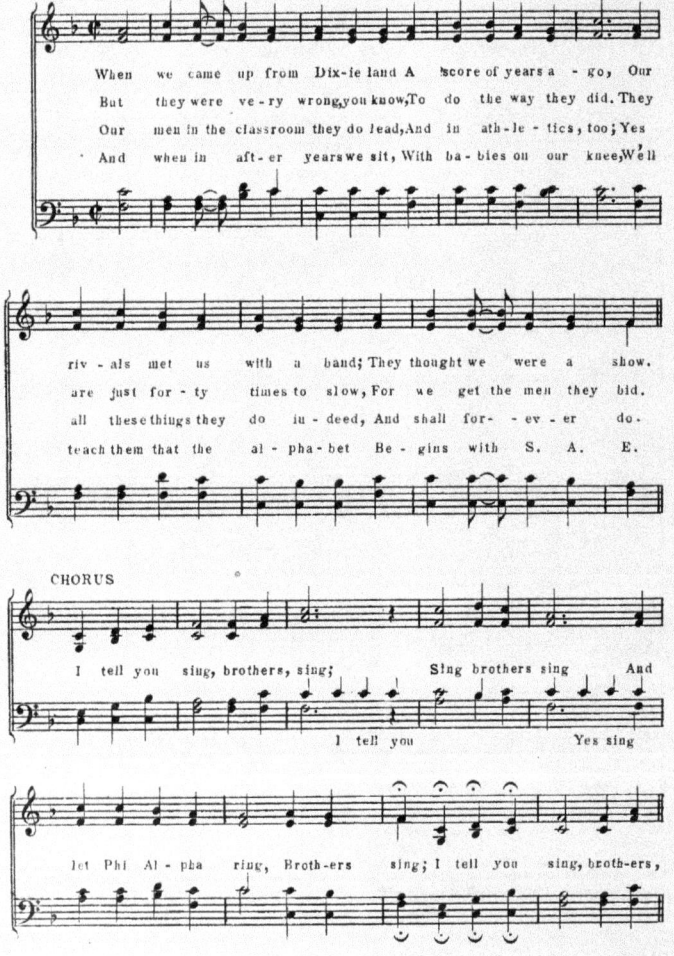

Tis said when Noah sailed in the ark,
  While others climbed a tree,
He let no men inside the boat
  But men of S. A. E.
Chorus.

Oh, Daniel in the lion's den
  Was happy as could be,
For the lions said we will not harm
  A brother S. A. E.
Chorus.

And when at last we're dead and gone
  To sail that fiery sea,
We'll twist the devil by the tail
  And yell for S. A. E.
Chorus.

Oh, Sigma Alpha Epsilon,
  And Sigma Alpha, too!
Where'er these names are heard in song
  There are some brothers true.
Chorus.

The credit for this song, one of the best the fraternity has belongs to George H. Kress and Alford K. Nippert, tho they should not be held responsible for others than the first three and the last verses.

DEAR S. A. E.

Tune: Die Wacht am Rhein

We meet to-night, as brothers, here, To worship what we each hold dear, And chant in sweetest mel-o-dy, Our love for our fra-ter-ni-ty.

Our sail-ors man the ship of State, From Plymouth Rock to Gold-en Gate, As to the breezes we un-fold Our flag of pur-ple and of gold.

Here let us pledge our faith a-new To Sigma's light we'll e'er be true, Her pre-cepts cher-ish in our heart Un-til the cord of life shall part.

CHORUS

Dear S. A. E.! How grand the cry! Our love for thee shall never die! Glorious, midst hon-ors gained and triumphs won, Firm stands the Sig-ma Al-pha Ep-si-lon.

PHI ALPHA

Tune: Red, White and Blue

H. C. Burger
Ohio Sigma

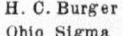

Oh, Phi Alpha, our badge plainly shows thee, Thy motto our founder well chose, With a wreath may we ever inclose thee, Through thee our loved order arose; All

Oh, Phi Alpha, thy deep-hidden meaning We ever shall keep in our mind, And to thee may we ever be leaning, In thee sweetest solace may find; We may

Oh, Phi Alpha, the future grows brighter, The fires of our friendship still burn, The clouds part, the sky grows the lighter, To thee may our hearts ever turn; Our

hail to the mot - to we cher-ish, May we
fol - low thy pre - cepts for - - ev - er, We
hopes and our fears and our du - ty, To

ev - er be strong and be bold, And thy teaching and truth nev - er
members of Sig - ma's true fold, Naught this bond of our un - ion can
thee e'er be lov - ing-ly told, Shine forth in thy strength and thy

perish, While we all wear the pur - ple and gold.
sev-er, While we all wear the pur - ple and gold.
beauty, While we all wear the pur - ple and gold.

THE FLAG OF SIGMA ALPHA EPSILON

Tune: March of the Men of Harlech

William C. Levere
Ill. Psi-Omega

Flag of gold-en hue and pur-ple Rip-pling in the breeze of hea-ven, Ral-ly we a-round thy col-ors Here we take our stand. 'Tis the flag of roy-al broth-ers, Flag that proud-ly flaunts all oth-ers, True our hearts, our

In the sun its splen-dor flash-es, And it waves 'mid thun-ders' crash-es Through the bil-lows sting-ing lash-es Still it floats on high. How it stirs each brave e-mo-tion! How it claims our heart's de-vo-tion! As it floats o'er

MY VOW

H. H. Cowan
Mich. Alpha

Tune: Maid of Athens

Sig-ma Al-pha Ep-si-lon Name I love to think up-on, Name a-
When home and friends I bade a-dieu For college life and comrades new, Sigmas
And when my col-lege days are o'er, And I have left their classic lore, Wher'er

bove all fair and dear, To loy-al Sig-mas far and near
then a-dopt-ed me In their fra-ter-nal fam-i-ly.
fate may cast my lot I hold in mem-'ry's brightest spot,

The vow I made so long a-go, Zo-a mus, sas a-ga-
This vow I made then bending low, Zo-a mus, sas a-ga-
The vow I made so long a-go, Zo-a mus, sas a-ga-

po. The vow I made, so long a-go, so long a-go.
po. This vow I made, then bending low, then bending low.
po. The vow I made, so long a-go, so long a-go.

HYMN OF COLLEGE DAYS

Tune: Austria

George Fullerton Evans

Mass. Gamma

Time flows onward ev-er on-ward, Bears us with it, though we'd stay,
Though we'd forswear all here aft-er For en-joy-ment of to-day.
Time will find us look-ing backward, Though the way be straight be-fore;
Time will find us mourn-ing pleasures Which may be en-joy'd no more.

Col-lege days will soon be memories, Bright, bright stars on darken'd skies,
But the love of col-lege friendships Is their light that nev-er dies.
Of all stars that light my jour-ney On-ward through E-ter-ni-ty,
Brightest is the con-stel-la-tion Of my dear Fra-ter-ni-ty.

SIGMA ECHOES

Tune: Massa's in the Cold, Cold, Ground

H. L. Feeman
Michigan Alpha

All my heartstrings are now beat-ing In tune to by gone time, Then my broth-ers I was meet-ing, Sing-ing Sig-ma's read-y rhyme. From my col-lege chums I've

Mem-'ry's mys-tic chords are quiv-'ring With words of long a-go. And I hear the old bell ring-ing At the eve-ning twi-light low; Voic-es chim-ing joy-ful

Pur-ple, gold and manhood roy-al, King-ly trin-i-ty, Bound the boys to liv-ing roy-al In the bonds of S. A. E. Years are gone and age is

A TOAST TO S.A.E.

Arnold D. Alt
Missouri Beta

Leo C. Miller
Missouri Beta

HOT GREEK SPORTS

Henry S. Bunting
Tenn. Zeta

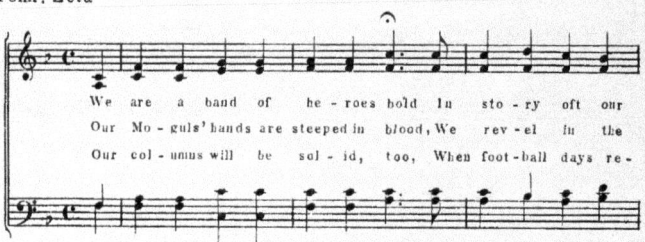

We are a band of he-roes bold In sto-ry oft our
Our Mo-guls' hands are steeped in blood, We rev-el in the
Our col-umns will be sol-id, too, When foot-ball days re-

deeds are told, All riv-als know that grand es-prit That
crim-son flood; Our clan de-lights in war's a-larms And
turn to view. Be vict-'ry with the red or blue Some

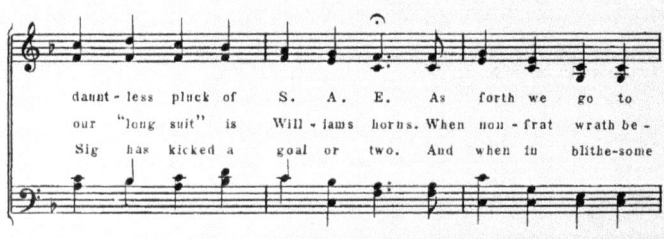

daunt-less pluck of S. A. E. As forth we go to
our "long suit" is Will-iams horns. When non-frat wrath be-
Sig has kicked a goal or two. And when in blithe-some

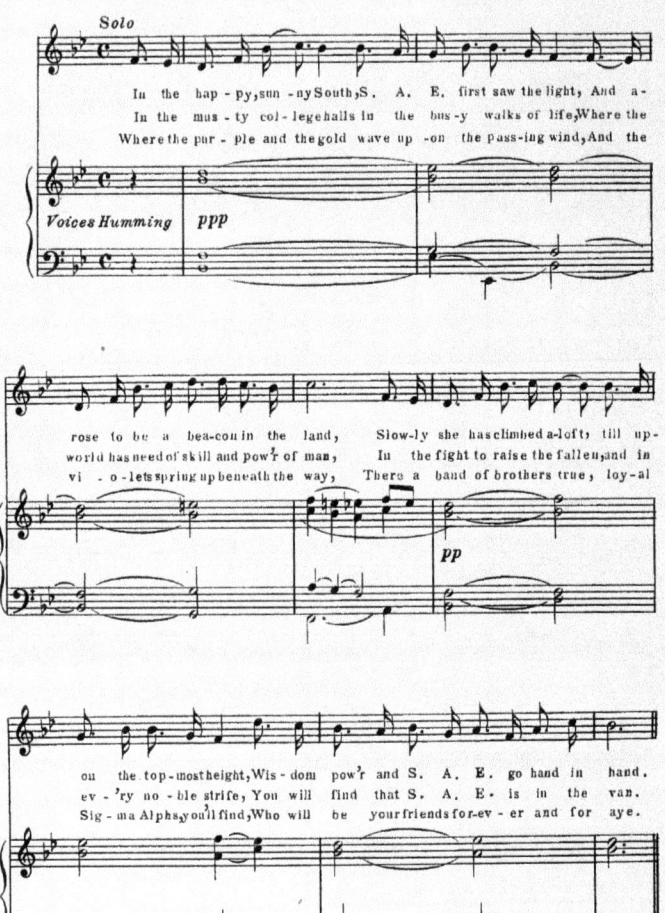

A HYMN TO S. A. E.

Tune: America

H. C. Burger
Ohio Sigma

Dear S. A. E. to thee, Our loved fra - ter - ni - ty,
Dear S. A. E. thy band, Of broth - ers no - bly stand,
Dear S. A. E. to thee, Bright star on life's dark sea,

Of thee we sing; Thy pur - ple and thy gold, Thy badge we
To guard and save. Tho' clouds ob - scure the sky, And light - nings
We lift our eyes. May all thy light be - true, Pure as the

love to hold, As em - blem of thy fold We tri - bute bring.
flash and fly, Thou rid - est safe and high Up - on the wave.
skies deep blue, And sweet as morn - ing's dew In Par - a - dise.

THROUGH THE YEARS

O. E. Boehymer
Indiana Alpha

Tune: Juanita

Fond - ly we treasure bliss-ful hours that take their flight,
Full be-yond measure are the joys to-night.
We will love thee ev'-er, in the days that are to be,
There is naught can sev-er our true hearts from thee.

When fan-cy, turning to the scenes that are no more,
Grows fond with yearning for the days of yore,
We will hold thee dear-er in the light of vanished years,
Thou wilt then be near-er through a vale of tears.

CHORUS

Sig-ma Al-pha Ep-si-lon we will wor-ship at thy shrine;
Loy-al, ev-er faith-ful, our hearts are thine.
Sig-ma Al-pha Ep-si-lon, Sig-ma Al-pha Ep-si-lon,
Hear us, while we pledge thee, till life be done.

EVER S.A.E.

Herbert H. Wiggin
Mass. Delta
Arr. for Male Quartet.

Tune: Lightly Row
A song for an Alumni Association

Arr. by *W. E. S.*

S. A. E., S. A. E., Here's a heart-y song for thee,
Far a - way, far a - way, Seemed the broth-er - hood of youth,
S. A. E., S. A. E., Joy of mer - ry col - lege days,

From our hearts, from our hearts, E'er the night de - parts.
But to - day, but to - day, We have learned the truth.
Un - to thee, un - to thee Be our ea - ger praise.

Dark - ness can - not hide our glee, We re - mem - ber joy - ful - ly
With a love that still shall be, Binds us our fra - ter - ni - ty,
Thou didst cheer us on our way, Taught us to love and o - bey

S. A. E., S. A. E., Ev - er S. A. E.
S. A. E., S. A. E., Ev - er S. A. E.
S. A. E., S. A. E., Ev - er S. A. E.

GATHERING OF THE CLANS

Tune: Maryland, My Maryland

William C. Levere
Ill. Psi-Omega

Brothers dear, we gather here,
Sigma Alpha Epsilon; With hearts so light and full of cheer,
Sigma Alpha Epsilon; We

We sing of thee these happy days,
Sigma Alpha Epsilon; We sing thy glory and thy praise,
Sigma Alpha Epsilon; We

We'll cherish thee forevermore,
Sigma Alpha Epsilon; Though scattered far on distant shore,
Sigma Alpha Epsilon; Our

THE PURPLE AND THE GOLD

Charles Allen Lloyd
Tenn. Nu.

Rev. E. E. Madiera
New York Sigma-Phi

LET'S PLEDGE OUR BANNER

Tune: Benny Havens, Oh!

Marcellus S. Whaley
Tenn. Omega

A DEFINITION

John Edward Russell
Ill. Psi-Omega

Walter E. Squire
Ill. Psi-Omega

WE DREAMED OUR ALUMNI WERE DEAD

Tune: My Bonnie Lies Over the Ocean

Henry Sydnor Harrison. New York, Mu.

Last night as we lay on our pil-low, Last night as we lay on our bed, Last night as we thought of our fut-ure, We dreamed our Al-um-ni were dead.

Last week with our house rent un-set-tled, Last week with our fac-es un-fed, Last week, when the treas-ury was emp-ty, We dreamed our Al-um-ni were dead.

Last month, when we wished a new man-sion, Last month, when we fig-ured a-head, Last month, when we sighed for ex-pan-sion, We dreamed our Al-um-ni were dead.

And when ev-er we need-er-as-sis-tance To be took by the hand and-er-led Then our plans usu-'ly meet this re-sis-tance We dream our Al-um-ni are dead.

1.-3. Oh, my, Oh, me, We dreamed our al-um-ni were dead were dead
4. Oh, my, Oh, me, We dream our al-um-ni are dead are dead

Bad dreams, night-mares; Oh, come back, Al-um-ni, to us.
Rum luck, bum luck, To dream our al-um-ni are dead.

CONVENTION SONG

Tune: Tenting on the Old Camp Ground

H. H. Cowan
Mich. Alpha

We're meet-ing to-night in con-ven-tion, boys;
Soon we'll fight the foe in the o-pen field
We too will part with a fare-well grip,

Gathered to-gether are we From the bus-y world with its
Fight in the bat-tle of life, But to-night we are boys, so
Just as the old-er boys, And out in the great wide

toil and care, We boys of S. A. E.
let us be Free from all care and strife.
world will be Tast-ing its cares and joys.

Man-y are the times that our hands have clasped!
Some of the fac-es that greeted us here,
But wheth-er or not we shall meet a-gain,

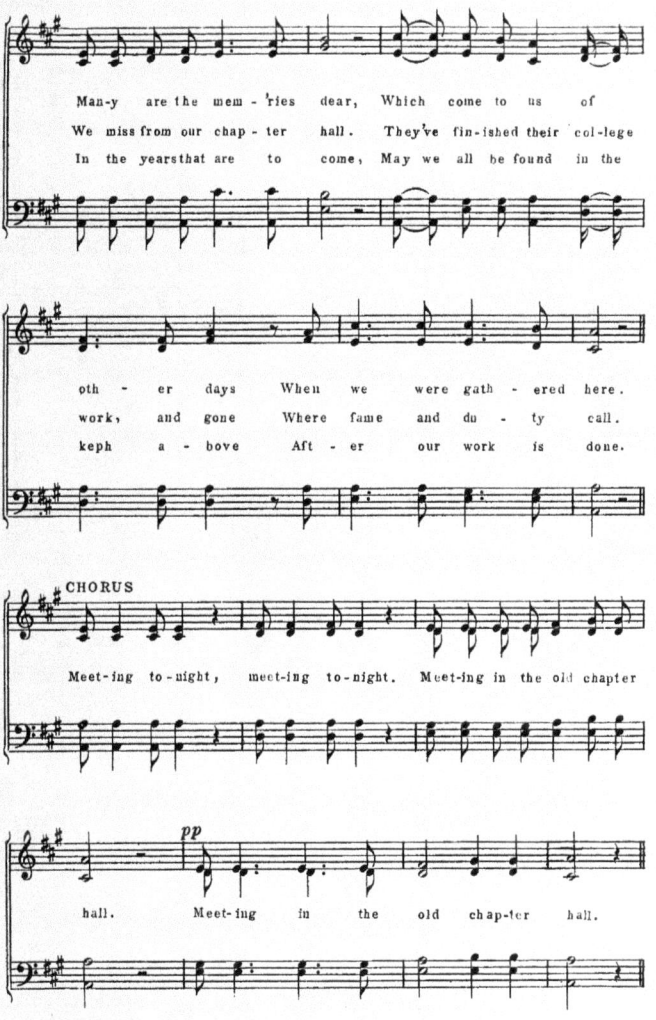

EVENING SONG

Tune: Stars of the Summer Night

William F. Giese
Wisconsin Alpha

Wher - ev - er far or near We sail up-
The joys we hour - ly learn Of sweet fra-
Wher - e'er our foot - steps roam, In sor - row
Then, broth - ers, here's to you! And here's to

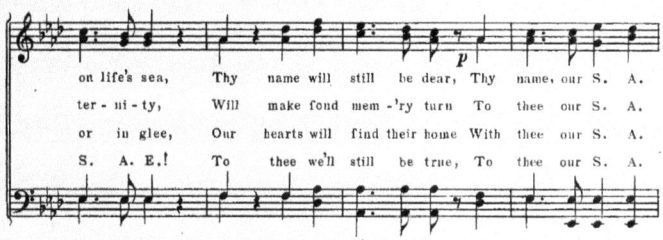

on life's sea, Thy name will still be dear, Thy name, our S. A.
ter - ni - ty, Will make fond mem - 'ry turn To thee our S. A.
or in glee, Our hearts will find their home With thee our S. A.
S. A. E.! To thee we'll still be true, To thee our S. A.

E. Thy name, Thy name, our S. A. E.
E. To thee, To thee, our S. A. E.
E. With thee, With thee, our S. A. E.
E. To thee, To thee, our S. A. E.

THE SPIRIT OF S.A.E.

William C. Levere
Ill. Psi-Omega

F. E. Abbott
Ill. Psi-Omega

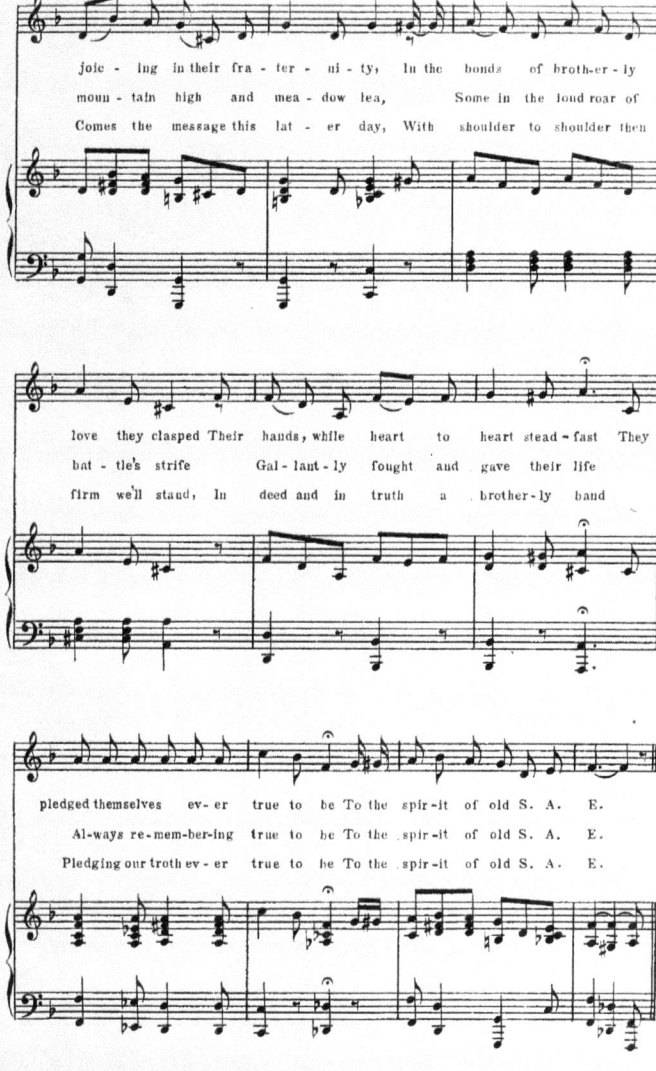

THE SPIRIT LOVED SO DEAR

Tune: Old Familiar Place

E. N. Wentworth
Iowa Gamma

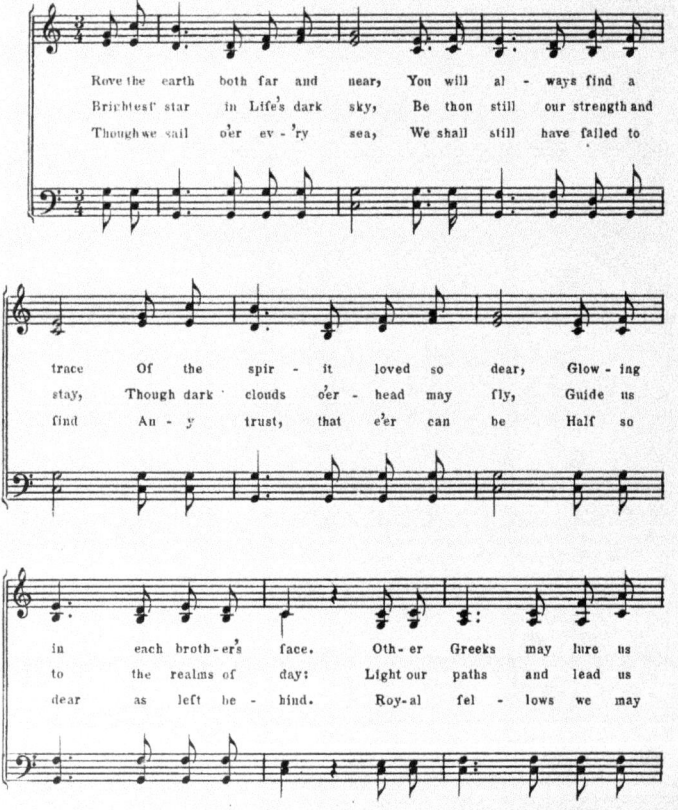

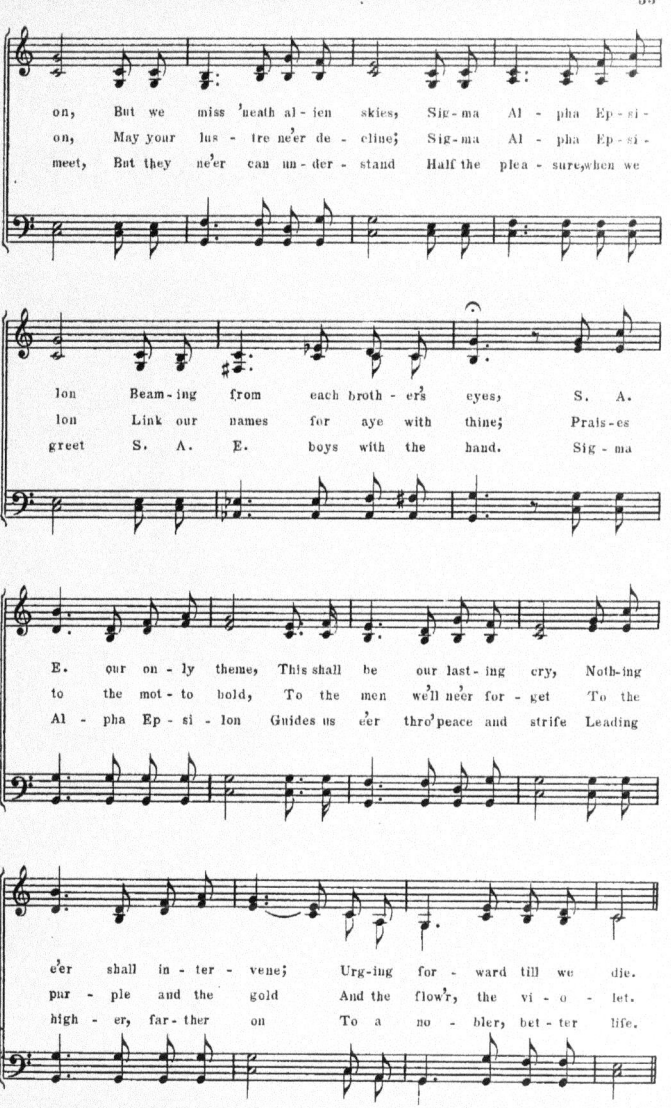

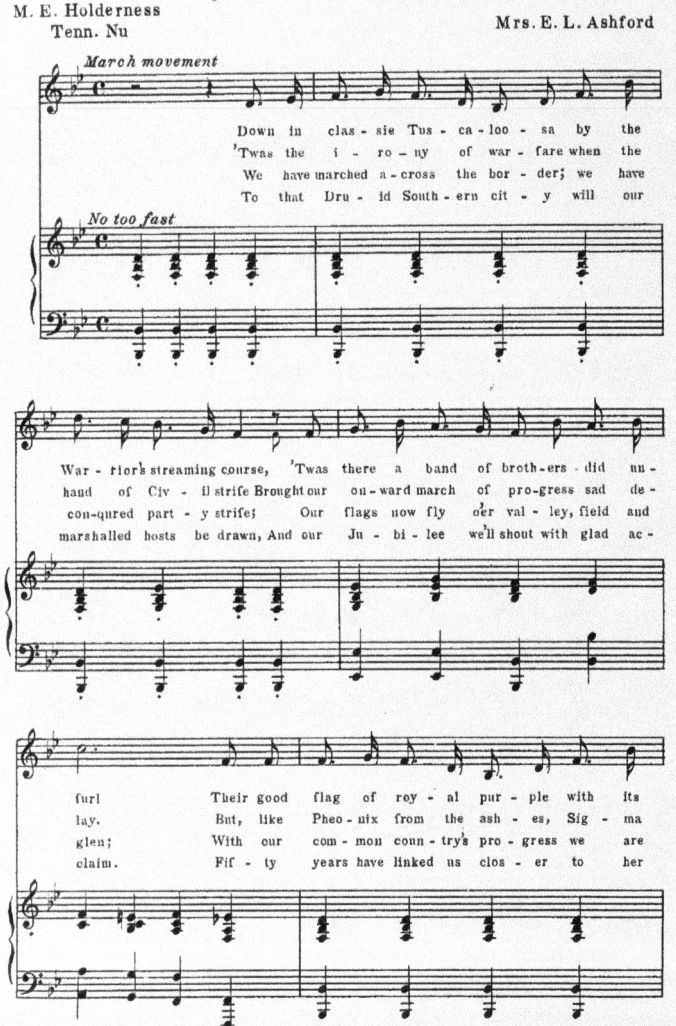

OCEAN TO OCEAN

Al. F. Leue
Ohio Epsilon

Newton Swift
Michigan Alpha

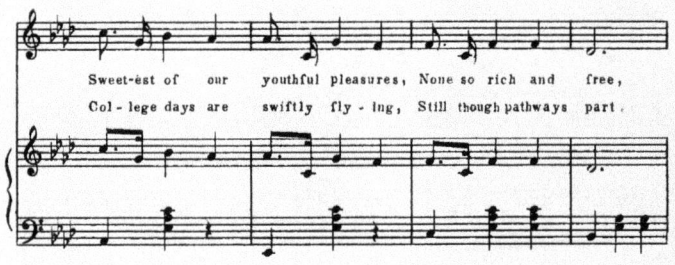

Sweet-est of our youthful pleasures, None so rich and free,
Col-lege days are swiftly fly-ing, Still though pathways part.

Choicest boon of col-lege treasures. Broth-er-hood in S. A. E.
Tru-est friendship nev-er dy-ing, Glows in ev-'ry brothers heart,

ALUMNI SONG

Tune: "Annie Laurie"

H. C. Burger
Ohio Sigma

IN PRAISE OF S. A. E.

Tune: Auld Lang Syne

AN ALUMNI HYMN

Tune: Frederick

Thomas McNider Simpson
Virginia Omicron

William C. Vail
Indiana Alpha

PARTING SONG

Tune: Old Black Joe.

Poco adagio

Sad-ly we wait as the part-ing hour draws near,
Some we may miss who are with us here to-night,
Slow-ly we turn from the hall we love so dear; When, Brothers, when shall our
Friends tried and true we have found them in the fight; When, Brothers, when shall our

band be gathered here To meet a broth-er-hood un-brok-en S. A. E.
scattered ranks u-nite, - To meet a broth-er-hood un-brok-en S. A. E.

CHORUS

We're part-ing; we're part-ing, Far, far we soon shall be, Ah,

when to meet at thy dear port-als, S. A. E.

BILLY GOAT SONG

Alfred Keister Mills
Colo. Zeta.

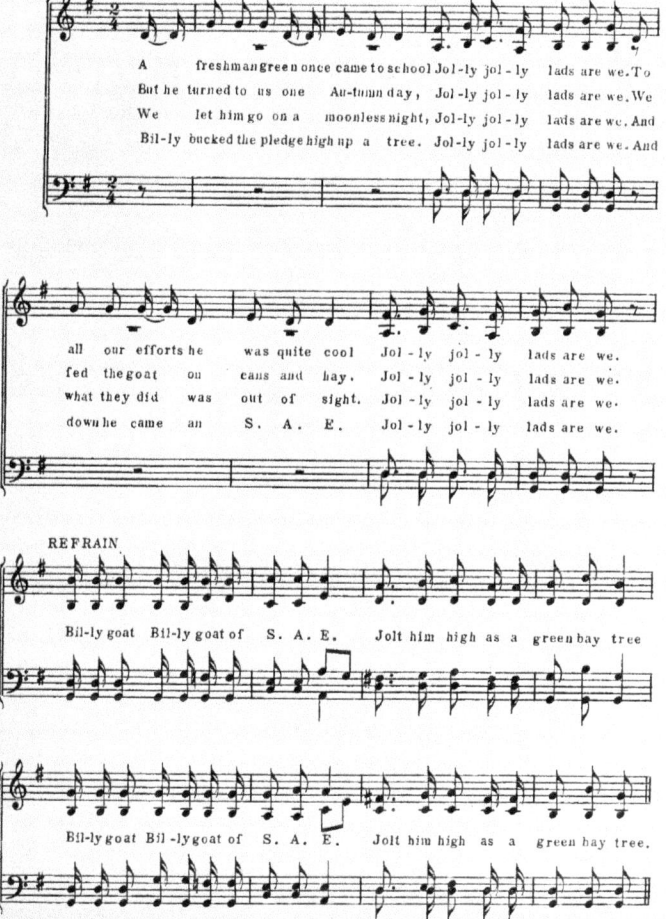

AVE ATHENA

From Schubert's Wanderer

By a Member of
Ohio Sigma

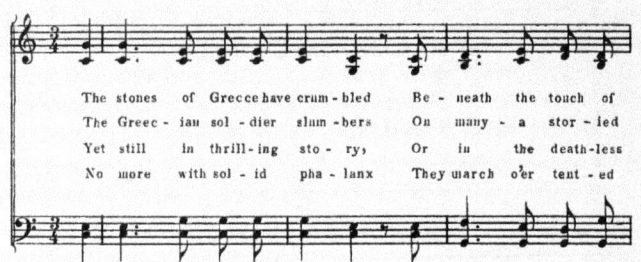

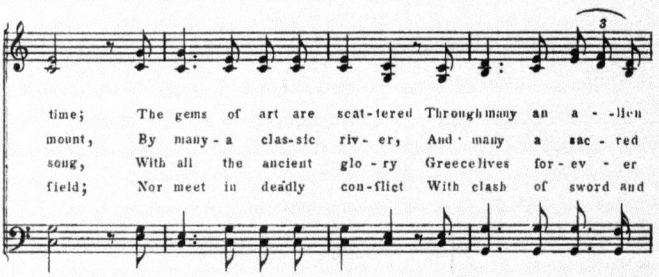

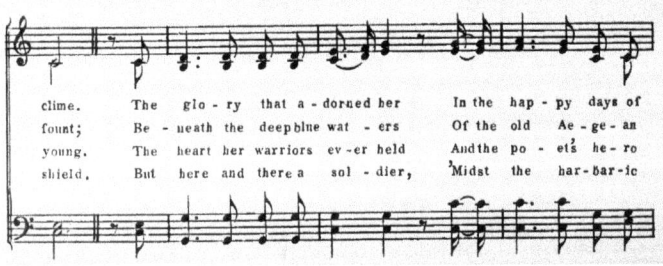

Hope H. Lumpkin
Tenn. Omega

FRATERS LOYAL

Tune: Clear the Way

Old S. A. E. is a jol-ly good frat, And a loy-al bunch you may bet your hat, And when they gath-er in a crowd, O you may hear their voic-es loud, say

And when we spike a like-ly lot, And for our ri-vals make it hot, O then is the time you hear us shout Min-er-va's men you can't beat out, so

So S. A. E. at the top will stand, In all the length of this great land, For on this rock we take our station Our bounds the con-fines of the nation, so

CHORUS

Fra-ters loy-al, tell the sto-ry, Fra-ters loy-al, tell the sto-ry, Fra-ters loy-al, tell the sto-ry, S. A. E. be e'er our glo-ry.

TO THE VIOLET

Champe S. Andrews
Alabama Alpha-Mu.

Dr. J. Holmes Mc Guinness
New York Sigma-Phi.

Dear, dainty vi-o-let, fair-est of flow'rs,
Steal-ing thy beau-ty in morn's ear-ly hours,
Co-quett-ing with sun-beams and kissed by thy show'rs.

'Tis thou art cho-sen to tell to the world That the
flag of De-Vo-tie will nev-er be furled Till the
last col-lege dome to the dust has been hurled.

In the language of flowers, true love is thy meaning;
And from thee thoughts divine may be had for the gleaning:
Aiding to live and from wickedness weaning.

Thou hast nature's own colors, the purple and gold,
More brilliant in beauty as autumn grows old
And strong forests tremble at winter's first cold.

In the autumn of life, Death would fain cut us down;
But we gaze in his face now, without fret or frown,
For tranquil are souls with a violet crown.

May we spread far and wide, in these states grand and free
The teachings embodied, dear Violet in thee;
And the world will then rise and bless dear S.A.E.

AS FROM COLLEGE WALLS

Tune: "My Last Cigar"

Scott C. Lyon
Tenn. Zeta.

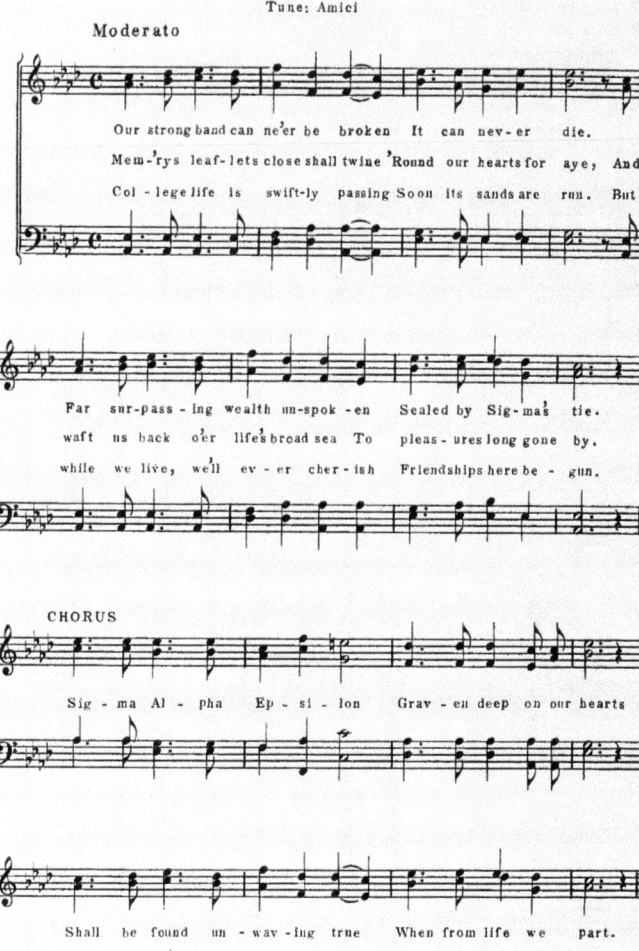

BANQUET SONG

Jos. Clemons
Penn. Sigma-Phi.

Tune: Bingo

3

Here's to S.A.E. drink her down, drink her down,
She was born in Tuscaloosa,
Drink her down, drink her down,
Drink her down, down, down.

4

Here's to each Alumnus drink her down, drink her down,
Here's to each Alumnus who has come to sup among us,
Drink her down, drink her down,
Drink her down, down, down.

5

Here's to all our ladies drink her down, drink her down,
Here's to all our ladies whose charms and smiles pervade us,
Drink her down, drink her down,
Drink her down, down, down.

THE ONLY ONE

K. F. Leet
Ohio Sigma

SINGING PHI ALPHA

W. W. Filkin
Kansas Alpha

Tune: The Bull Frog

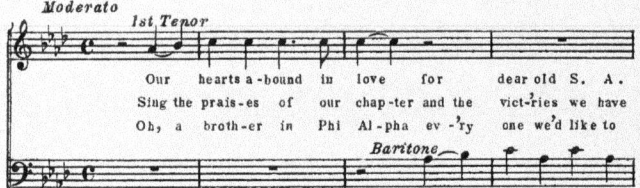

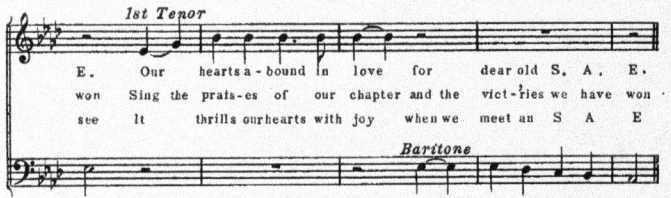

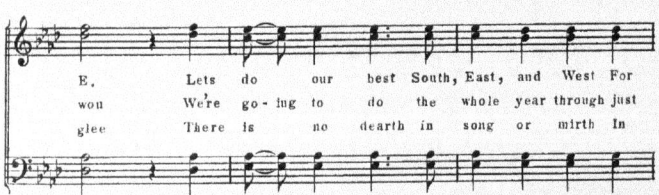

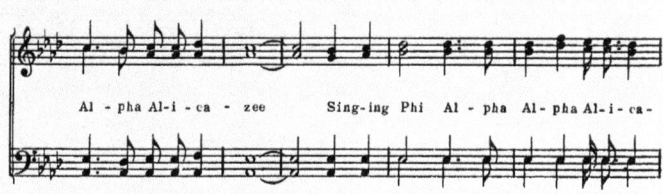
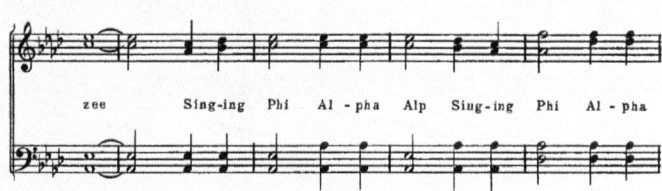

THE BANNER OF OUR BROTHERHOOD

Tune: Ben Bolt

Words by O. L. Hall
Ill. Psi-Omega

Arr. by W. S.

The fold, roy-al fold, of the pur-ple and gold That
The ban - ner that's kiss'd by the warm South - ern breeze, That
The vi - o - lets bloom in the val - ley, Sig Alph, The

flut - ters from moun-tain to sea   Now re-calls the old vows and the
flut - ters in winds of the west   That greets ev-'ry sun - rise on
gold - en - rod nods on the plain   And we stand by the shield of Min-

EVEN THE STARS SPELL S. A. E.

George Shidler
Neb. Lambda-Pi.

Tune: Twinkle, Twinkle Little Star

Twin-kle, twin-kle lit-tle star, S. A. E. spells from a - far,
Twin-kle, twin-kle lit-tle stars From Con-ven-tion com-ing far.
Flash-ing, flash-ing, shoot-ing star, Whisper to me from a - far

Up a - bove the world so high Like a dia-mond in the sky.
Weak my limbs each sound but jars, Show me how to reach a car.
That a cer-tain girl loves me, That she too loves S. A. E.

CHORUS

Twin-kle, twin-kle lit-tle star Now we know just what you are

Then the freshman in the dark Thanks you for your ti-ny spark He

could not tell which way to go If you did not twin-kle so.

OLD S. A. E.

Tune: Beside the Mill

N. W. Gratz
Kentucky Epsilon

THE S. A. E. GOAT

William C. Levere
Illinois Psi-Omega

Tune: Bridal Chorus from Lohengren

Hail to the Goat With yawn-ing throat, As he ad-vanc-es with no-ble tread! His whisk-ers steam, And his teeth gleam, Well does he know he's a-bout to be fed. Vic-tims a-dore him! Bow at his shrine! Make him be-lieve he's real-ly sub-lime. Pray for the best! Pre-pare for the rest! The best you can hope for is six months in bed.

How he does dance! Rare high and prance! Let loose his teth-er and give him a chance. Hear that low growl Come from his jowl, There is a scare in his hyp-not-ic glance. Mer-ci-ful Pet-er! Saints do for-fend! By his wild actions we are near-ing the end. One moment more, He'll close his jaw, Freshmen you'll lose the seat of your pants.

He loves to chaw! Dotes on red gore! Rel-ish-es freshmen when they are green! Bites cob-ble stone! Chews hu-man bone! Smiles ve-ry sweet-ly and licks his chops clean. Loud-ly her trumpets! Kneel, Vic-tim Kneel! If he should hurt you just let out a squeal. T'will soon be o'er, Tat-tered and tore, You'll go to the an-gels for change of scene.

GOOD NIGHT, BROTHERS

Jos. Clemons
Penn. Sigma-Phi.

Pledge to the ladies,
We're going to leave you now.

Farewell, brothers,
We're going to leave you now.

IN 1856

Edward Mellus
Mass. Gamma

Music arr. by
Millard F. George

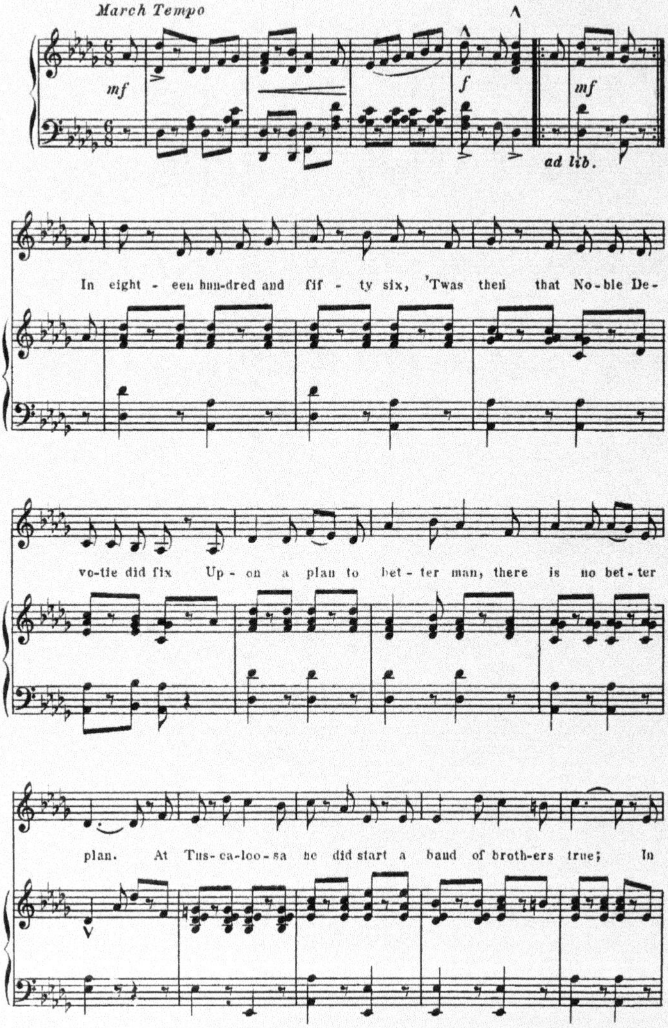
March Tempo
mf
f
mf
ad lib.
In eight - een hun-dred and fif - ty six, 'Twas then that No-ble De-
vo-tie did fix Up - on a plan to bet - ter man, there is no bet - ter
plan. At Tus-ca-loo-sa he did start a band of broth-ers true; In

A TOAST TO S.A.E.

Will Riley
Phil Macbride
Iowa Beta

Phil Macbride.

We pledge a toast to ev-ery broth-er
Let oth-er frats in oth-er schools sing

loy - al   And drink his health wher - ev - er he may
prais - es   Of Delt - a U., Phi Gam., or D. K.

Copyright, MCMVII, by Phil Macbride.

106

Edwin N. Ferdon
New York Alpha

THE COLORS I ADORE

Tune: My Old Kentucky Home

CHEERING SONG

Morton Mc Nutt Prentis
Missouri Alpha

SIGMA ALPHA EPSILON HYMN

Tune: Portuguese Hymn

Adopted by D. P. Deatrick
Pennsylvania Delta

Our Father in Heaven, Creator of all, O source of all wisdom, On Thee would we call. Thou only canst guide us And cause us to

But vain must the aim of Fraternity be, Unless its ennobling, And mindful of Thee. Then pour forth Thy spirit, And ever pro-

In ev'ry condition In sickness, in health, In poverty's vale, or Abounding in wealth, At home or abroad, on The land on the

E'en down to old age, may
Our friendships all prove
But ripened by time to
Unchangeable love;
And then when the years shall
Our features remold,
May such bonds of friendship
Our children enfold.

Our fair S A E, will
Thou strengthen her days
To send forth forever
True sons to Thy praise;
O widen her borders,
Extend her fair fame,
And let all the glory
Redound to Thy Name.

OLD DAYS OF CHARM

Tune: The Heart Bowed Down

E. E. Madeira
New York Sigma-Phi.

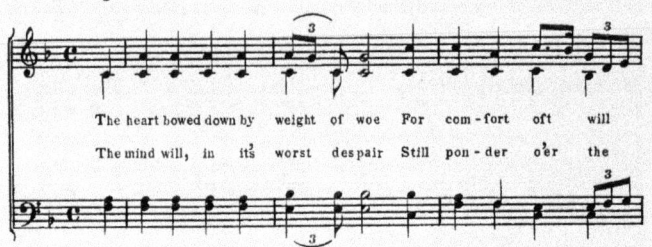

The heart bowed down by weight of woe For com-fort oft will
The mind will, in its worst despair Still pon-der o'er the

fly To hap-pier days of long a-go Whose
On mo-ments of de-light, that were Too

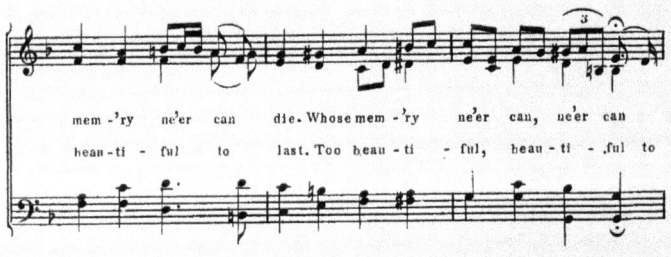

mem-'ry ne'er can die. Whose mem-'ry ne'er can, ne'er can
beau-ti - ful to last. Too beau-ti - ful, beau-ti -,ful to

YOU ARE PLEDGING LEFT AND RIGHT

Tune: Are You Going to the War, Willie Boy!

Adolph George Pierrot
Illinois Theta

OUR COLORS

Newton E. Swift
Michigan Alpha

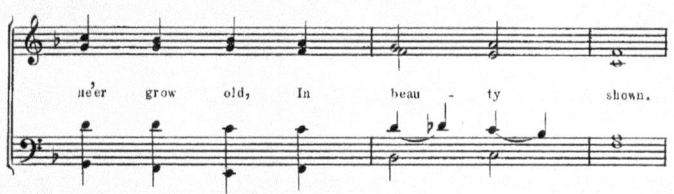

CHORUS *Allegro*

SONG TO MINERVA

T. C. Hempelmann
Missouri Beta

Tune: Forsaken

JOIN IN THIS OUR SONG

Tune: Spanish Melody

THE BOYS OF S. A. E.

Newton E. Swift
Michigan Alpha

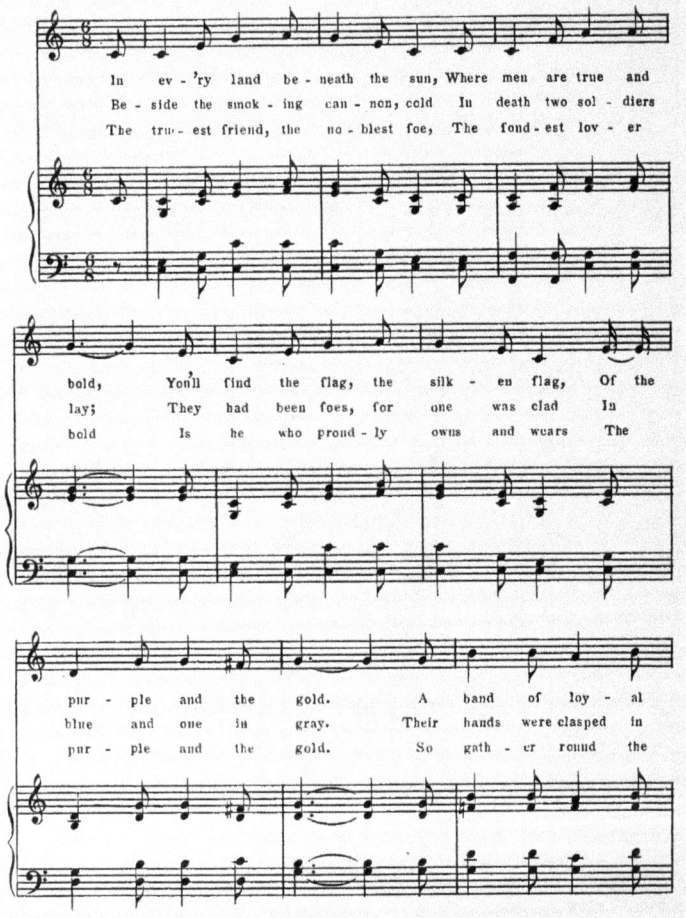

JOIN ALL BROTHERS

Tune:- Nut Brown Maiden

J. B. Strauss
Ohio Epsilon

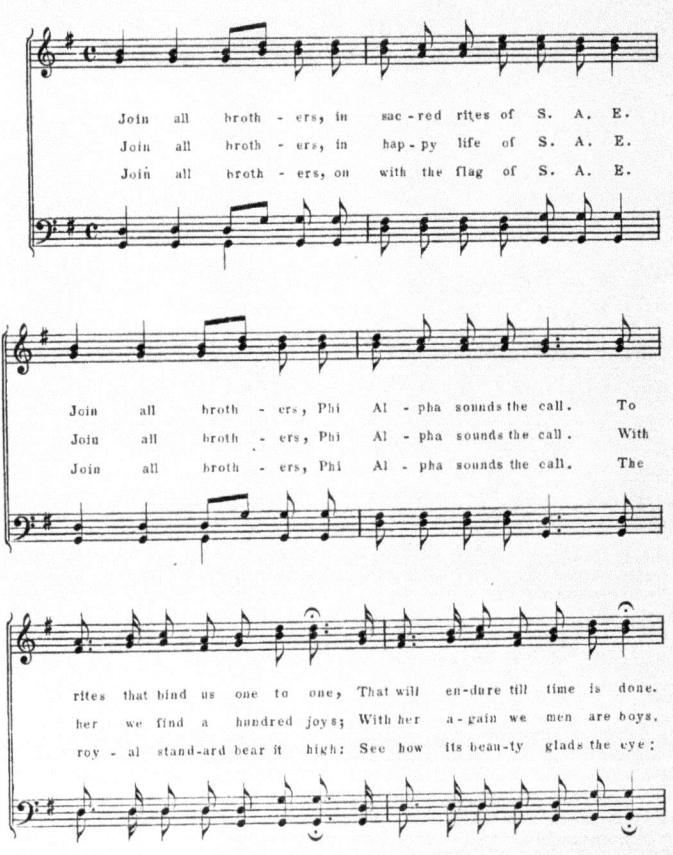

Join all brothers, and closer draw to S.A.E.
Join all brothers, Phi Alpha sounds the call.
Her name and fame, protects them well,
With you the victory will dwell.
Join all brothers, and closer draw to S.A.E.
Join all brothers, Phi Alpha sounds the call.

Join all brothers, join in a health to S.A.E.
Join all brothers, Phi Alpha sounds the call.
May still her glory greater grow,
And e'er a stain her history know.
Join all brothers, join in a health to S.A.E.
Join all brothers, Phi Alpha sounds the call.

SIGMA ALPHA EPSILON.
March.

Melbourne Clements.
Ill. Theta.

A DIXIE ECHO.

Dedicated to S.A.E.

Claude M. Stauffer.
Penna Sigma-Phi.

* Chord last time only.

THE GEORGIA BETA.

MARCH and TWO-STEP.

C. S. Connerat Jr.
Georgia Beta.

The March of the Eminent Archon.

K. F. Leet.
Ohio Sigma

THE ILLINOIS PSI-OMEGA MARCH

F. E. Abbott.
Ill. Psi-Omega.

VARSITY DAYS.
Introducing the
MICHIGAN DRINKING SONG.

C.M. Foss.
Ohio Theta.

MICHIGAN DRINKING SONG.

MAZURKA IN G MINOR.

Walter Squire.
Ill. Psi-Omega.

INDEX TO TITLES.

			PAGE.
An Alumni Hymn	Thos. McN. Simpson	Va. Omicron	63
Alumni Song	H. C. Burger	Ohio Sigma	60
As from College Walls	Scott C. Lyon	Tenn. Zeta	72
Ave Athena	By a member of Ohio Sigma		66
Awakening, An	Adolph G. Pierrot	Ill. Theta	97
Banner of Our Brotherhood, The	O. L. Hail	Ill. Psi-Omega	86
Banquet Song	Jos. Clemons	Pa. Sigma-Phi	80
Beacon Song, The	Charles S. Reinhart	Ohio Epsilon	28
Billy Goat Song	Alfred K. Mills	Colo. Zeta	65
Boys of S. A. E., The	Newton E. Swift	Mich. Alpha	126
Cheering Song	Morton M. Prentis	Mo. Alpha	107
Colors I Adore, The	Edwin N. Ferdon	N. Y. Alpha	106
Come, Boys, Come	Shearon Bonner	Tenn. Lambda	11
Convention Song	H. H. Cowan	Mich. Alpha	48
Dear Old S. A. E.	W. C. Vail	Ind. Alpha	1
Dear S. A. E.			7
Definition, A	{ John Edward Russell Walter E. Squire }	{ Ill. Psi-Omega }	44
Dixie Echo, A	Claude M. Stauffer	Pa. Sigma-Phi	133
Encircled in the Purple and Gold	Marvin G. Mason	Pa. Sigma-Phi	40
Evening Song	William F. Giese	Wis. Alpha	51
Even the Stars Spe'l S. A. E.	Geo. Shidler	Neb. Lambda Pi	89
Ever S. A. E.	Herbert H. Wiggin	Mass. Delta	345
Fairest, The	{ John Edward Russell Walter E. Squire }	{ Ill. Psi-Omega }	98
Flag of Sigma Alpha Epsilon	William C. Levere	Ill. Psi-Omega	12
Fraters			76
Fraters Loyal	Hope H. Lumpkin	Tenn. Omega	70
Gathering of the Clans	William C. Levere	Ill. Psi-Omega	36
Georgia Beta March and Two-step	C. S. Connerat, Jr.	Ga. Beta	136
Good Night, Brothers	Jos. Clemons	Pa. Sigma-Phi	96
Good Night Song	H. S. Harrison	N. Y. Mu	75
Greeting Song	Newton E. Swift	Mich. Alpha	121
Heigho Song	By Tenn. Omega		122
Hot Greek Sports	Henry S. Bunting	Tenn. Zeta	26
Hurrah Song	F. W. Pierpont	Mich. Alpha	90
Hymn of College Days	George F. Evans	Mass. Gamma	19
Hymn to S. A. E.	H. C. Burger	Ohio Sigma	30
Illinois Psi-Omega March, The	F. E. Abbott	Ill. Psi-Omega	144
In Classic Tuscaloosa	{ M. E. Holderness Mrs. E. L. Ashford }	Tenn. Nu	56
In 1856	Edward Mellus	Mass. Gamma	100
In Praise of S. A. E.			62
Its S. A. E.	Wassell Randolph	Tenn. Kappa	120
Join All Brothers	J. B. Strauss	Ohio Epsilon	128
Join in This Our Song			125
Let's Pledge Our Banner	Marcellas S. Whaley	Tenn. Omega	42
Light of S. A. E., The			41
Live On! S. A. E.	Joseph C. Walker	Tenn. Lambda	118

			Page.
March of the Eminent Archon, The	K. F. Leet	Ohio Sigma	140
Mazurka in G. Minor	Walter E. Squire	Ill. Psi-Omega	161
Minerva Waltzes, The	Walter E. Squire	Ill. Psi-Omega	147
My Vow	H. H. Cowan	Mich. Alpha	14
Name We Love, The	{ MacAllister Moore / Edward H. Virgin }	Mass. Gamma	83
Ocean to Ocean	{ Al. F. Leue / Newton Swift }	Ohio Epsilon / Mich Alpha	58
Ode to a Fraternity Brother	{ N. L. DeVotie / Philip L. Scantling }	Ala. Mu / Wash. City Rho	4
Old Days of Charm	E. E. Madeira	N. Y. Sigma-Phi	112
Old S. A. E.	N. W. Gratz	Ky. Epsilon	92
Only One, The	K. F. Leet	Ohio Sigma	82
Our Colors	Newton E. Swift	Mich. Alpha	147
Parting Song	William C. Veil	Ind. Alpha	64
Phi Alpha	H. C. Burger	Ohio Sigma	8
Pledge Song	Al. F. Leue	Ohio Epsilon	94
Purple and the Gold, The	{ Charles A. Lloyd / Rev. E. E. Madeira }	Tenn. Nu / N. Y. Sigma-Phi	38
S. A. E. Bonds	E. N. Wentworth	Iowa Gamma	15
Sigma Echoes	H. L. Freeman	Mich. Alpha	20
S. A. E. Goat, The	William C. Levere	Ill. Psi-Omega	93
S. A. E. Violets	George D. Kimball	Colo. Zeta	25
Sigma Alpha Epsilon March	McEnerne Clements	Ill. Theta	130
Sigma Alpha Epsilon Hymn	D. P. Deatrick	Pa. Delta	108
Sigma Alpha Epsilon Polka	Newton E. Swift	Mich. Alpha	157
Sing Brothers, Sing	{ Geo H. Kress / A. K. Nippert }	Ohio Epsilon	2
Singing Phi Alpha	W. W. Filkin	Kans. Alpha	84
Song of Devotion	Hope H. Lumpkin	Tenn. Omega	110
Song of Loyalty, A	Alfred K. Mills	Colo. Zeta	78
Song to Minerva	T. C. Hempelman	Mo. Beta	124
Spirit Loved so Dear, The	E. N. Wentworth	Iowa Gamma	54
Spirit of S. A. E., The	{ William C. Levere / F. E. Abbott }	Ill. Psi-Omega	52
Toast, A	Edward H. Virgin	Mass. Gamma	50
Toast to S. A. E., A	{ Leo C. Miller / Arnold D. Alt }	Mo. Beta	22
Toast to S. A. E., A	{ Will Riley / Phil MacBride }	Iowa Beta	102
Through the Years	O. E. Boehymer	Ind. Alpha	31
To Sing Thy Praise	C. W. Stowell	Maine Alpha	46
To the Violet	Champe S. Andrews	Ala. Mu	71
Varsity Days	C. M. Foss	Ohio Theta	153
We Dreamed Our Alumni Were Dead	H. S. Harrison	N. Y. Mu	47
We Lift Our Voices	Oliver E. Boehymer	Ind. Alpha	74
We'll Live for Thee	{ Newton Swift / Joseph Clemons }	Mich. Alpha / Pa. Sigma-Phi	32
We Pledge Our Love to Thee	T. McNider Simpson	Va. Omicron	77
When a Thousand Years Are Gone	H. S. Harrison	N. Y. Mu	18
While Warm the Life Blood Flows	Geo. M. Harton	Mich. Alpha	68
Whistle, The			164
You Are Pledging Left and Right	Adolph G. Pierrot	Ill. Theta	114

INDEX TO FIRST LINES.

	PAGE.
A freshman green once came to school	65
All my heart strings are now beating	20
A student sat in his room	118
As from the college walls we go	72
As I was walking down the street	122
Brothers all 'neath the folds of the purple and gold	78
Brothers dear we gather here	36
Come boys, come! let us sing	11
Come brothers, listen and you will hear	107
Come brothers, join our singing	41
Come gather round and let us sing tonight in royal glee	62
Come let us love thee while warm the life blood flows	68
Come now brother Sigs and let us sing our song of love	83
Dear dainty violet, fairest of flow'rs	71
Down in classic Tuscaloosa	56
Dear S. A. E., to thee our loved fraternity	30
Dear Sigma Alpha Epsilon, we pledge our	77
Dixie Echo, A	133
Far through the years that have guarded thee	110
Flag of golden hue and purple	12
Fondly we treasure blissful hours that take their flight	31
For Sigma Alpha Epsilon, a song for S. A. E.	38
Georgia Beta March	136
Good night, brothers	96
Greeting Phi Alpha, one and to all	121
Hail to the goat	93
Here's to S. A. E.	80
How bright was the day	63
How e'er seem the moments of onspeeding time	49
If in the days when hope is lost	15
I know not whence it rises	97
I know we must part yet united in soul	4
Illinois Psi-Omega March	144
I'm pledged to dear old S. A. E.	94
In eighteen hundred fifty-six	100
In every land beneath the sun	126
In the happy, sunny south	28
Join all brothers in sacred rights of S. A. E.	128
Last night as we lay on our pillows	47
Let's pledge our banner, brothers	42
March of the Eminent Archon	140
Mazurka	161
Minerva the Goddess	124
Minerva Waltzes, The	147
My friend, to you I sweetly pray	44

	PAGE
Of all the fairest flowers	98
Oh now the woods and meadows gay	25
Oh Phi Alpha	8
Oh Sigma Alpha Epsilon	46
Old S. A. E. is a jolly good frat	70
Our college days are over	60
Our Father in Heaven	108
Our hearts abound in love for dear old S. A. E.	84
Our knightly banner grandly floats	90
Our strong band can ne'er be broken	76
Rove the earth both far and near	54
Royal purple and old gold	117
Sadly we wait as the parting hour draws near	64
She's the queen of our devotion	1
Sigma Alpha Epsilon fraters join in this our song	125
S. A. E., S. A. E. Here's a hearty song for thee	34
Sigma Alpha Epsilon March	130
Sigma Alpha Epsilon, Name I love to think upon	14
Sigma Alpha Epsilon Polka	137
Soft purple clouds edge the crimson of the west	106
Sweet and low, Sweet and low	45
Sweetest of our youthful pleasures	58
The boys were gathered in the chapter hall	52
The fold, royal fold of the purple and gold	86
The heart bowed down by weight of woe	112
The stones of Greece have crumbled	66
There are some dear Greeks and we love them all	120
Time flows onward, ever onward	43
Twinkle, twinkle, little star	83
'Varsity Days	135
We are a band of heroes bold, We lift our hearts and voices to thee	26
Well, here's to Sigma Alph	22
We'll sing S. A. E., old S. A. E.	18
We'll sing a song for S. A. E.	82
We lift our voices and our hearts to thee	74
We part from thee, our halls so dear	32
We pledge a toast to every brother loyal	102
We meet to-night as brothers here	7
We're meeting tonight in Convention, boys	48
We're seated round the festive board	50
When twilight gently, slowly steals	92
When we came up from Dixie land	4
Wherever far or near we sail upon life's sea	51
Whistle, The	164
You are pledging left and right	114

Lightning Source UK Ltd.
Milton Keynes UK
UKHW011039210820
368606UK00003B/463